THE GIFT WITHIN ME

The Struggle That Made Me

Ginger Pittman

Table of Contents

Dedication

This book is dedicated to the people whose love, strength, prayers, and presence carried me through every storm and lifted me into my purpose.

To my children - Karderius, Keonna, and Kywra-you are my heartbeat, my strength, and my greatest blessings. Everything I build is for you.

To my grandbabies - Khy'lan, Kaiden, and Ka'Mari - my K-Squad. Your joy, laughter, and innocence brighten every corner of my life. You are the future of this empire.

To my husband, Nakia - my backbone, my partner, my protector, my peace, and the love God aligned with me. Thank for standing beside me, believing in me, and helping me rise above every struggle Your loyalty made me stronger.

To my mother, Vernell Anita Harvey, who gave me life, strength, and foundation. Your love molded me into the woman I am today.

To my sisters and brothers –

Faye, Pamela, Aariona, Maurice, Kristy, Karl Jr., Kristopher, and Danielle - each of you is part of my story. Our shared blood, struggles, and history helped shape my resilience and identity.

To my father, Karl Lee Cleaves, resting in peace - I pray every accomplishment honors your name.

Your spirit travels with me through every chapter of my journey.

THE GIFT WITHIN ME

To Geraldine Thompson and Lester Thompson, my husband's grandparents – thank you for treating me and my children with genuine kindness, respect, and love throughout this marriage. Your warmth, acceptance, and goodness were blessings I will always cherish.

To my aunts and uncles -

Aunt Constance, Aunt Angie, Uncle Famous, and Uncle Glynn - your wisdom, guidance, and prayers have been anchors in my life. Thank you for your support and presence through the years.

To my nephew, Rafael Cleaves - thank you for always stepping in when I needed you, especially at the last minute. Your loyalty and willingness to be there made a real difference in my life.

To Christopher, also known as Carlito, thank you for always taking part in my projects, supporting my ideas, and standing behind me in everything I involve myself. Your encouragement has been a blessing on my journey.

To Danielle Hines – thank you for being there for my daughter, my grandkids, and myself. Your support, love, and presence helped carry us through moments that would have been much harder without you.

To Jarrika Evans – thank you for your support, your involvement, and your willingness to stand with me and my family. Your presence has meant more than words can express.

To my circle of true friends and real supporters –

Kae Briggs, Patricia Hayslett-Simmons, Andrea Tucker-Talley, , Katelyn Thompson, (just know your role has no limit, family),

THE GIFT WITHIN ME

Toriane Carruthers, Latoya Chism, Cheryl Campbell, and Vincent (Doc) –thank you for being my listening ears, my encourage when life felt heavy.

Acknowledgments

I thank God for the spiritual gifts and strength He has given me to endure my experiences.

Introduction

Some gifts you choose. Some gifts choose you.

My gift didn't whisper; it woke me, shook me, broke me, and rebuilt me.

From the moment I entered this world, God made it clear I wasn't born to walk an ordinary path. He marked me with a number that symbolizes foundation, stability, and destiny.

But destiny doesn't arrive wrapped in comfort. It arrives wrapped in struggle.

And every struggle I survived carved the foundation—

for *Black Magic Productions*...

for my ministry...

for my liquor line...

for my clothing brand...

for my spiritual business...

for every single thing.

Love Ties

Love ties, but it has no time.
The measurements of faith we often try to dictate,
some may even plan.
What is it we look for in a perfect woman or a perfect
man?

Misunderstandings leading to hurt and cries.
I love you today, but three hours later,
I have to say my goodbyes.
Was it you, or should I take the blame?
Hurt is hurt, but the love feels the same.

A strike of the fist.
Belittlement in front of family.
Physical abuse, now it's domestic violence.

I love you indeed, but this shit is toxic.
The day you left, I damn near lost it.
Tried to overdose, but I knelt in my prayer closet.
I spoke with God, the Spirit said, "Stop it."

You're a boss. You have your own path.
Any man who finds you has found a gold mine ahead.
Raise your head and straighten that crown.
He walked away; his head should be down.

You're the gift that stands out in the treasure box,
The precious diamond that was once lost.

- Written by Ginger D Pittman for
Katherine Walker for a boost of love
and strength...

Chapter 1
Early Childhood & Spiritual Gift Awakening

I came into this world marked by the number 4, born on April 4th at 4:00 AM, weighing 4 pounds and 4 ounces. A divine signature, a spiritual imprint, a quiet message from God:

This child is different.

My mother, Vernnell, held me in her arms and said my eyes didn't look like a newborn's. They were alert, watching, following things she could not see. My father, Karl, sensed early that I was born with a knowing, a sensitivity far beyond my age.

I grew up between two sisters — Faye, older, and Pamela, younger — all born so close together that we were practically stair steps. But even as toddlers, our energies were different. They played with dolls and toys. I played with shadows and silence. I felt emotions that weren't mine. I woke from dreams that came true. I walked into rooms and felt who had argued in them hours before.

Children aren't supposed to carry that kind of weight. But I did.

Before I knew the meaning of the word "gift," I knew what it felt like. I could feel when someone was lying. I could sense when something bad was about to happen. I saw movement in corners nobody else noticed. I would freeze, stare, and follow spirits with my eyes long before I could even talk.

My family didn't understand it. They didn't push it away either, but they couldn't guide me. They just watched me grow into something they couldn't name.

I wasn't just a child.

I was a vessel.

And even in my innocence, I knew it.

Chapter 2
Family Roots, Pain & Separation

Family is supposed to feel like home. But my childhood home was complicated.

There was love — good moments, laughter, and warm memories — but there was also tension, secrets, arguments, and emotional distance. My parents tried their best, but they carried their own traumas. My siblings and I were close in age, but we were raised in emotional storms none of us knew how to name.

My father was hard-working, disciplined, and gifted in his own way. My mother was strong and resilient, but weighed down by life. Their marriage cracked during my early years, eventually splitting completely. Their divorce split more than a marriage; it split our whole foundation.

I learned early that family love doesn't always look like softness.

Sometimes it looks like quiet rooms.

Sometimes it looks like cold hallways.

Sometimes it looks like pretending everything is okay when it isn't.

I never hated my childhood, but it shaped me with truths I had to carry into adulthood. The roots that grew me were mixed:

love and pain, closeness and distance, joy and wounds.

The emotional separation that began in my childhood would echo through my relationships for decades. I grew up fast emotionally because childhood never gave me a chance to stay soft.

Chapter 3
Growing Up Fast: Motherhood At 15, 16 & 17

While other girls my age were getting ready for dances and school events, I was getting ready for motherhood. I had three babies by 17, each one born into a world of struggle and love.

People judged me, whispered about me, and doubted me, but motherhood became the anchor that kept me from drowning.

I held them close through nights of hunger, nights of fear, nights of praying I could give them what I never had: stability, safety, and unconditional love. I learned how to stretch a dollar and comfort a crying baby at the same time. I learned how to pretend I wasn't scared so they wouldn't be.

I became a warrior because I had no choice. Motherhood forced me to find a strength inside myself I didn't know existed. Every bottle, every diaper, every tear, every moment of fear shaped me.

I didn't get to be a teenager. I became a mother instead. And that responsibility, that love, saved me from paths that could have destroyed me.

Chapter 4
The Poison Scare That Changed Everything

Sometimes parenting becomes a battlefield you never expected.

One day, in a cold, run-down house we could barely heat, we relied on a kerosene heater to stay warm. The only container available was a Sprite bottle, a mistake waiting to happen.

My son, just a baby, drank from that bottle.

The world stopped.

Fear hit me so hard I could barely breathe. I raced to the hospital, praying, crying, begging God not to take my baby from me. I replayed every second in my mind, blaming myself, terrified of losing the child who depended on me.

But when the doctors ran tests, nothing was found. Not a single trace.

It was like God Himself said, "No. Not this child. Not today."

I walked out of that hospital understanding that my children were protected by a force stronger than anything I could see.

That moment changed me as a woman, a mother, and a

spiritual being. I became even more aware of my gifts — the intuition, the visions, the knowing. And I became even more protective, determined to create a life safer than the one I had been forced to endure.

Chapter 5
Abuse, Survival & Escape

Love shouldn't hurt, but my early relationships did.

I found myself trapped in cycles of abuse, manipulation, jealousy, and violence. I endured controlling partners who smiled in public and changed behind closed doors. I hid bruises behind makeup. I silenced cries behind smiles. I walked on eggshells in my own home.

It wasn't weakness. It was survival.

Every abusive moment taught me a lesson: what love is *not*. Some men used their fists. Some used their words. Some used manipulation so deep it felt like a spell.

And I stayed longer than I should have, because when you grow up in survival, you learn to tolerate pain as if it is normal.

But trauma ages you. It wears your spirit thin. It makes your heart tired.

One day, I looked in the mirror and didn't recognize myself. That's when I started planning my escape, one step at a time, one moment of courage at a time.

I didn't leave because I stopped loving them. I left because I finally started loving myself.

Chapter 6
The Kidnapping & Silent Cries For Help

One of the darkest moments of my life came when fear became a prison.

I was kidnapped, taken away from safety by someone I once trusted. He controlled my movements. He controlled my fear. He controlled my choices.

A cousin helped him, watching the door as if guarding my freedom were a crime.

They took me to an old house, hidden and silent. Fear sat heavy on my chest, but so did survival. I knew I had to think, not panic.

I used clues and quiet signals to reach help. I contacted someone who understood me well enough to read between the lines. My spirit guided me through that moment, whispering what to say, how to move, how to stay alive.

When help finally came, it was like the breath I had been holding finally released. I survived something meant to break me.

But trauma doesn't leave quietly. For years, I slept with the light on. For years, my body reacted to certain noises. For years, I stayed alert even when I was safe.

That moment didn't destroy me. It awakened something

stronger inside me: a deeper intuition, a louder spiritual sense, a sharper inner voice.

I learned that survival is a skill, and I mastered it.

Chapter 7

The Engagement & the Double Life

I thought an engagement meant clarity. Commitment. Truth coming to the surface instead of hiding in the dark.

I was wrong.

By the time he proposed, my children's father had already married another woman.

A whole double life — fully formed, fully active — while standing in front of me pretending we were building a future. I did not know it yet, but people around him did. And slowly, the truth started finding its way to me through whispers and warnings.

The first real hint came from his aunt's husband. He came to my house, sat with me, and spoke carefully, like a man who knew he was about to shake the ground beneath my feet. He told me to check things out for myself. Told me everything I needed to know without saying too much. His tone wasn't malicious; it was cautionary. That was enough.

I called to the courthouse to confirm it. I checked the records myself. Page numbers. Dates. Documentation. Just like he said, it was all there in black and white. A marriage already in place. No confusion. No misunderstanding. No technicality. The truth was printed, stamped, and undeniable.

I reached out to the wife. But even after the truth came out, even after I made contact with her, he did not disappear. He still came to my house. Still showed up uninvited. Still fought. Still argued. Still acted like he had control over me while legally belonging to someone else. Exposure did not stop him. It only made him bolder.

I got tired. Tired of the chaos. Tired of the fighting. Tired of a man bringing destruction wherever he went.

That exhaustion is what pushed me to move to Memphis. Not fear. Not heartbreak. Fatigue. I needed distance. I needed clarity. I needed peace.

But even Memphis did not stop him. He followed me there, claiming he had gotten an annulment. Swearing it was over this time. Swearing he had handled it. Swearing I could finally trust him.

Smart as I am, I watched patterns instead of words. I noticed how he suddenly started walking to the store instead of driving. Over and over again. He had a phone, but those walks gave him time. Time to escape. Time to call her. Time to tell lies about where he was, claiming he was working with a cousin or running errands.

Patterns don't lie.

I contacted her again. This time, she didn't just listen. She came. And when she did, he left with her.

No explanations. No closure. No final argument needed. The truth had already finished speaking. That was the moment the double life collapsed completely, not because I fought for answers, but because I trusted my discernment.

That engagement taught me a lesson that shaped every relationship after it.

Love without honesty is a trap. Commitment without truth is control. And a double life always exposes itself.

I didn't leave broken; I left aware.

Chapter 8
Becoming an Exotic Dancer to Survive

Survival does not always come wrapped in dignity. Sometimes, it comes wrapped in judgment.

By the time I made the decision, I wasn't chasing dreams or excitement. I was chasing stability, food, bills, and a way to keep my children safe without asking anyone for help who had already proven they couldn't be trusted.

I became an exotic dancer because I needed money. Not fast money for luxury. Not money for attention. Money to *survive*. There is a difference, even if people refuse to see it.

When my mother found out, her disappointment came quickly. Her judgment came even faster. She did not hide how she felt. She questioned my choices and my character. Questioned the woman she thought she raised. Her words stung, but I understood where they came from. Mothers carry expectations. They carry fear. They carry shame that does not always belong to them.

At first, all she could see was the title. *Exotic dancer.* She did not yet see the responsibility behind it. She did not yet see the discipline. The boundaries. The control. The fact that I was doing what I had to do without leaning on anyone else.

Then the money came. Not slowly. Not inconsistently. It

came steady. I paid bills. I provided. I handled business.

And suddenly, survival looked different through her eyes. When she saw that I could shower her with gifts, that I was no longer struggling the way I had been, her judgment softened. Survival has a way of changing people's opinions when it proves itself effective.

She even took me to the mall. We shopped together for dance outfits, shoes, things she never imagined she would be helping me choose. The same woman who had once judged the decision was now participating in the process. That moment wasn't about approval; it was about understanding. She saw that I was not reckless. I was resourceful.

That chapter of my life taught me something I never forgot. People will judge your methods until they benefit from your outcomes. They will question your choices until they see your strength. And they will speak loudly about morality while quietly enjoying the comfort your sacrifice provides.

I did what I had to do. I did not lose myself in it. I did not let it define me. I did not stay longer than necessary. It was a season, a tool, a bridge. And when I crossed it, I kept moving forward without apology.

Chapter 9
Returning Home, 13 Charges & Spiritual Protection

When I moved back home, it wasn't with celebration. It was with awareness. I returned to my hometown hoping familiarity would bring peace, but old places remember you. They remember your strength, your past, and your capacity to survive. Sometimes, they test you the moment you step back into them.

Not long after I returned, trouble found me. It started with an altercation at an apartment complex. Words escalated. Emotions flared. Energy shifted fast. What should have ended quietly didn't. Gunfire broke out, loud enough to shake walls and spirits alike. Fear spread quickly, and once police lights hit the pavement, the narrative no longer belonged to the truth. It belonged to assumptions.

Before I could process what was happening, I was facing thirteen charges. *Thirteen.* I understood immediately what that meant. Not just legally, but spiritually. I knew the system did not need me to be guilty to punish me. I knew how quickly a woman like me could be swallowed whole if I relied on logic alone.

So I didn't. I went spiritual. I did not leave my fate in the hands of the court system by itself. I worked black magic deliberately and intentionally. Not out of anger. Not out of revenge. Out of protection. Out of survival. Out of knowing exactly who I am and what my gift can do when activated.

I prayed, but I also worked. I did spiritual work. I called on ancestral protection. I set intentions with precision. I did what I have always done when my life was threatened. I used black magic.

People misunderstand that phrase because they want to. They think it means darkness, harm, or chaos. For me, it meant control. It meant balance. It meant justice. It meant shifting energy where the system was designed to crush me. I did not panic. I did not beg. I did not break.

Every charge disappeared. All thirteen of them. No conviction. No record. No residue. Just silence.

People asked how I walked away untouched. I did not explain myself. I never do. Power does not require confession, and protection does not ask permission.

That moment changed everything. It was no longer possible for me to pretend my gift was coincidence. It was no longer possible to downplay what I was capable of spiritually. I stopped hiding behind softer language to make other people comfortable. Black magic saved me. It protected my freedom. It preserved my future.

I did not beat thirteen charges by luck; I beat them by power.

Chapter 10
Music: Lil Gin & My Return To The Stage

Long before films, long before the spiritual business, long before *Black Magic Productions*, there was music. Music was my first voice, my first outlet, my first calling.

I performed in the early 2000s, when Memphis music was rising, raw, gritty, and real.

I shared stages with legends:

- Mystikal
- Yo Gotti
- La Chat
- Playa Fly
- Mac E
- Don Trip
- Kurtis Blow
- and many more from the Memphis scene

I was known as *Lil Gin*, a fierce young woman with a powerful presence and no fear of the mic. Back then, the clubs were packed, the speakers shook the ground, and I felt alive in a way nothing else could match.

But life pulled me away — motherhood, abuse, survival, trauma, healing, responsibilities, and spiritual battles took center stage. Still... the music never left me. It stayed in my spirit, waiting for the right time.

And in 2025, the stage called me again.

I released *"Standing On Business"* and *"Highway to Hell."* These songs weren't just tracks; they were testimonies. War stories. Resurrection. Declaration of everything I survived.

Lil Gin wasn't dead. She was reborn — wiser, stronger, spiritual, unstoppable. Music became another pillar of my empire.

My journey in music was not small; I shared space with big names who respected my grind.

When I performed alongside Memphis legends, I learned that the industry is cutthroat; talent matters, but ambition matters more; and jealousy can come fast, but respect only comes from authenticity.

Yo Gotti brought the crowd. La Chat brought the rawness. Playa Fly brought the street wisdom. Mac E brought charisma. Don Trip brought fire. And I stood there among them — a young woman with kids, trauma, pain, and strength — but I held my own.

Those nights proved something to me: I wasn't just a survivor; I was born to be seen, heard, and respected. It was around 2004 when most of this happened, and I carved my name into that history.

Even if life pulled me away for years, those performances fueled the fire that would later push me into films, ministry, business, and entrepreneurship.

Chapter 11

Marriage #1: Derrick's Secrets & Betrayal

Derrick entered my life during a time when I wanted stability. He was handsome, thought he was prettier than me, and charming enough to make me believe that things could finally get better.

But lies have a way of revealing themselves.

He told me he had no kids. I believed him. Then one phone call to his job shattered that lie. The person on the phone referred to me as "the baby mama."

My heart dropped.

Everyone at his job knew he had a child, except me.

The betrayal burned. It wasn't just the lie. It was the disrespect.

When confronted, Derrick spiraled. He grabbed a belt and tried to hang himself from the ceiling. I had to stop him — physically stop him — from taking his own life.

Then he hid in a closet inside a cardboard box, mentally collapsing under the weight of his own lies. I had to call Mobile Crisis to get him help.

Marriage wasn't supposed to look like this — chaos, fear,

THE GIFT WITHIN ME

lies, and emotional breakdowns. Our marriage lasted only a year, but it left enough wounds to last a lifetime.

I learned that some men don't want love; they want ownership, attention, and a woman who will shrink herself to keep them comfortable.

But I refused to shrink.

Chapter 12

Warren & Georgia: Promises, Lies & Escape

After so many broken relationships, Warren seemed like a breath of fresh air at first. He treated me like royalty, at least in the beginning.

I moved to Warner Robins, Georgia, with him around 2005, hoping for a new start, a new life, and the stability I had been craving for years. For a while, it felt like I had finally gotten it right. The home was nice. The treatment was gentle. The promises felt real.

But promises don't always match a person's heart. Hours turned into whole nights with him never coming home. Lies started slipping through the cracks. Patterns of disrespect began revealing themselves.

My intuition, the same gift I had tried to silence for years, started screaming. He disappeared for long stretches, ignoring calls, leaving me alone with my kids in a state where I had no family, no friends, and no support.

The queen treatment turned into neglect. The love turned into distance. The calm turned into confusion.

One day, I called my father in Memphis and said, "Daddy, I can't stay here." He didn't hesitate. He got in his vehicle, drove the hours, loaded up everything but a single chair, and took me home.

That drive was my freedom ride. I left that relationship with dignity — not broken, not afraid, but aware.

Warren showed me the final lesson I needed: If a man cannot stand beside your spirit, he doesn't deserve your presence.

Georgia was a chapter, not a lifetime.

Chapter 13
Depression, Hotel Nights & Rebuilding Strength

Depression doesn't always look like sadness. Sometimes, it looks like strength stretched too thin. Sometimes, it looks like a mother holding her tears in so her kids don't see her break. Sometimes, it looks like staying in hotel rooms because you have nowhere else to go… but still keeping your kids fed, clothed, and safe.

There were nights when the weight of everything became too heavy — the failed marriage, the abuse, the disappointments, the betrayals, the loneliness, the fear.

I slept in hotel rooms with my kids, pretending it was a "mini vacation," when, in truth, it was survival. I stared at cracked ceilings, wondering how my life had gotten so far from what I dreamed. I fought with myself emotionally, spiritually, and mentally because giving up was never an option.

In those moments, God sat quietly with me. He didn't speak loudly. He didn't shake the earth. He just kept breath in my body and strength in my bones.

My kids never saw me break. They saw me push. They saw me rise. They saw me fight through depression with a power I didn't know I had. That season rebuilt me, not quickly, not easily, but piece by piece, tear by tear, prayer by prayer.

Hotel rooms became stepping stones. Depression became direction. And weakness became the soil where my strength grew back.

Chapter 14
Marriage #2: Shaun, Prison Walls & DV

Shaun was familiar, someone I grew up with. That familiarity may have made me ignore the red flags at first. But prison changes people, and not always for the better.

He came into my life with scars from his past. Attempted murder charges. A hardened heart. A violent spirit.

Arguments were loud, sharp, and often dangerous. We fought, literally. There was a night when we both ended up in jail because survival meant defending myself. His mother played a part in his cheating, creating a cycle of disrespect and dysfunction.

I wanted stability. He wanted control.

There was a moment when my mother picked him up after an argument, carrying his clothes down the street like she was rescuing him instead of helping us fix our marriage. Things only got worse from there.

The breaking point came the day of the car.

I had bought him a classic — a 1979 Cordoba. An antique. Valuable. Something I was proud to give him. Instead of asking questions, instead of coming inside to understand, he walked in angry. Accusatory. Loud. I dangled the keys in his face, trying to show him it was his.

We fought. Not verbally. Physically.

Glass tables shattered in my living room. Furniture moved. Rage filled the space where peace was supposed to live. My children, still in elementary school, witnessed things children should never see. They tried to intervene. One of my daughters called the police.

That still sits heavy in my chest.

After the fight, Shaun got into the shower. I was beyond reason. Beyond fear. I threw a blow dryer over the shower rod, trying to electrocute him. Not because I was calculating. Because I was overwhelmed, angry, and living in survival mode.

When the police arrived, they saw the bruises on him. They did not see the history. They did not see the provocation. They did not see the years of escalation.

I was arrested.

I was transferred from jail to Fayette County, where I was from. I remember telling the sheriff, half exhausted and half honest, that they must be tired of seeing me because I do black magic and I do not stay locked up. And I meant it.

I worked magic again. Quietly. Intentionally. Without panic. I stayed in jail only a few hours. Charges faded. The system loosened its grip. I walked out again without consequences sticking.

That marriage ended not because I failed, but because it was never built on safety. Jail cells cannot fix a violent spirit. Love cannot heal a man who refuses accountability.

THE GIFT WITHIN ME

When Shaun and I separated, it was final.

What followed was worse.

Chapter 15
The Organization & The Danger

After Shaun and I separated, my life did not suddenly become peaceful. It became dangerous.

We eventually moved, but not right away. We stayed for a while. I remember how one of the guys had already shot up the house where the grandparents were staying. I walked down there myself and got the baby mama out of the house, putting her up against a tree. At that point, we still didn't leave.

I wasn't pretending or posturing. Emotions were high, and the situation was dangerous. She was part of the opposition. Shots had already been fired. They had shot my car while my daughter was getting ready to go to the store, with my kids inside.

I went down to their house, and that's where everything reached a breaking point. It was made clear that this could either turn into an all-out war that dragged on for weeks, or it could stop right there. In that moment, everything had to shut down before it went any further.

Not long after, I became involved in a Vice Lord organization. Let me be clear. This was an organization, not a gang, the way people like to label it. It was originally structured around community, protection, and unity. What outsiders see is chaos. What insiders sometimes try to create is order. The problem is that violence infiltrates anything when power gets involved. I stayed on the safer side of it. I tried to keep things focused on protection and structure, not destruction.

My daughter became initiated while she was still in high school. That still weighs on me. It really does. At the time, it felt like protection. It felt like alignment. It felt like keeping her safe in an unsafe environment.

But environments change. Opposition moved in. Crips. They moved into the area, and tension followed. Disrespect escalated. Threats were made openly. Guns were pointed in the street. Names were called. Lines were drawn without my consent.

One of the younger ones, hot-tempered and reckless, shot up an opposition house after being disrespected. That act put everyone in danger. Including my household.

I did not hide. I walked into the middle of it.

Gunfire. Chaos. Adrenaline.

I went directly to the opposing house and knocked on the door to make amends. I explained that an underage kid had acted out of emotion. I took responsibility where responsibility needed to be taken, because retaliation would have meant bodies. I made it clear that peace had to happen, not later, but immediately.

That moment stopped a war from escalating further. People think survival always looks like running. Sometimes, survival looks like standing still in front of danger and refusing to let it grow.

That period of my life taught me this: when violence surrounds you, neutrality is not an option. Leadership is. Accountability is. Wisdom is.

Eventually, I walked away from that life completely. Not because I was weak, but because I was evolving. I had already survived too much to let chaos be my ending.

That chapter of my life did not destroy me; it sharpened me.

Chapter 16
Marriage #3 Chunsey: Chaos, Familiarity & Another Lesson in Survival

When Chunsey entered my life, chaos was already surrounding me. I was living in survival mode, moving from place to place, navigating danger, tension, and environments where peace was never guaranteed. Violence was close. Decisions carried weight. Every move mattered.

He was connected to the same environment I was trying to manage. He was around during the period when conflicts were spilling into the streets, when arguments did not stay verbal, and when danger had a way of pulling people in whether they asked for it or not. I was in another relationship at the time, but chaos does not respect boundaries.

The moment everything collided was a fight that got out of hand.

I was already angry, already overwhelmed, already operating on adrenaline. The situation escalated fast, and before logic could catch up, things turned physical. Chunsey heard about it and rushed toward the scene, but instead of driving, he grabbed his nephew's bike and rode it up there.

That alone should have told me everything.

He fell off the bike on the way and had to be taken to the hospital. At the same time, I ended up needing medical attention myself after the fight. We were both in the hospital for different reasons, connected by chaos instead of intention.

That moment became the beginning.

Chunsey was familiar. He was present. He showed concern when things were intense. In a life where danger had become routine, familiarity felt like comfort. I mistook availability for stability and presence for peace.

We moved forward quickly.

The relationship turned into a marriage, not because it was grounded, but because everything around us was unstable. When you are constantly surviving, you sometimes cling to whatever feels solid in the moment, even if it is not built to last.

Chunsey was not a bad man. But he was not the man I needed. He was tied to environments I was already trying to outgrow. He existed comfortably in chaos while I was beginning to feel the weight of it. Where I was becoming more aware, more discerning, more spiritually alert, he remained rooted in patterns that no longer served me.

The marriage did not last. There was no dramatic ending, no single breaking point. Just a slow realization that this union was another lesson, not a destination. I had married familiarity instead of alignment. I had chosen comfort over clarity.

That marriage taught me something important. Not every man who shows up in the middle of your storm is meant to stay once the skies clear. Some people enter your life because you are wounded, not because you are ready.

Chunsey was part of my journey, but he was not part of my future. Marriage number three closed a chapter for me. Not with bitterness, but with understanding.

Chapter 17
Darrian: Church, Drums & Disappointment

Before I met Nakia, there was Darrian — the church drummer. Our relationship felt different because it was wrapped in church culture. At first, it felt safe. It felt purposeful.

We attended Bible study, Sunday services, choir practices, and youth programs together. He played the drums with passion, and people admired him. We were in church every Wednesday and Sunday, trying to build something spiritually grounded.

But spirituality doesn't automatically make someone accountable. Behind the church, there were doubts, inconsistency, and emotional distance. His baby mama became a constant problem — drama, jealousy, arguments, interruptions, negativity. She didn't just affect him... she affected us.

Some of his family liked me. Some tolerated me. But his love wavered. His loyalty cracked. But what he lacked in commitment, he made up for in small experiences. He was the first man, before Nakia, to show my kids a different kind of happiness: trips to Nashville, beach outings, family moments that felt whole for a while.

But happiness without consistency is an illusion, and eventually, the illusion broke.

Darrian taught me an important truth: A man can be in the

church and still not be ready for love.

So when he couldn't show up for me emotionally, I had to walk away spiritually.

Chapter 18
Meeting Nakia – The Man, The Hustle, The Heart

By the time Nakia came into my life, I was exhausted. Not physically, but spiritually. My heart had been pulled, torn, stitched up, ripped again, and still had to keep beating because my kids needed me.

When I met him, I wasn't looking for a man. I wasn't looking for love. I wasn't looking for anything but peace and a way to survive another day without falling apart.

I met Nakia on Facebook. Simple message. Simple conversation. Nothing dramatic at first. But from the beginning, there was effort. Real effort. The kind you feel before you fully trust it. The kind that makes your heart flutter just enough to pay attention.

I told him the truth early. I told him I was not about to spend hours on the phone with someone I was not serious about. He laughed, thought it was a game, but he stayed on the phone anyway. An hour passed fast. When I said it was time to get off the phone, he said, "I thought we were in a relationship."

That told me something about him. He was smooth, but he was also present.

When we met in person, the first thing he said was that he thought I would be taller. I told him his neck was long. People always think I am taller than I am. I am four-foot-eleven and a half, and I own every inch of it. From that first meeting, he never really left.

Nakia was working at Buffalo Wild Wings when I met him. He did not have much money, but what he did have was consistency. The little money he made helped keep food in our house. When there was not enough, he did what he felt he had to do. He stole food so we could eat. He was not proud of it. He was not loud about it. He did it because he loved me and because nobody else was stepping up.

There was a day early on when I got hurt mowing the yard. I hit a hole, the mower snapped back, and I went down. When Nakia came from work, still in his Buffalo Wild Wings uniform, he took off his shirt, grabbed the equipment, and finished the entire yard without saying a word. Not for praise. Not for attention. Just because it needed to be done.

When he opened my refrigerator and saw how empty it was, he did not embarrass me. He did not ask questions. He made sure from that day forward that my kids and I had food. That was the beginning of our real partnership.

But Nakia was not perfect.

He tried to be slick at first. Facebook became a problem. One day, while he was at work, I noticed his phone vibrating in the dresser drawer. He had left it at home by mistake. The phone was lighting up nonstop. When I looked, I saw him texting me and another woman back to back.

When he came home, I confronted him. I hit him and he restrained me, but he never fought back. He held me because he knew I was angry, not dangerous.

That was the moment I set the boundary. If we were going to continue, Facebook had to go. No debates. No negotiations. He deleted it. Not because I forced him, but because he understood that my intuition was not something to play with. He knew by then that when I saw something, it was already exposed.

There was another moment when he was supposed to bring food home and did not. He was downtown with his sister and brother, having fun. I was furious. I told him to get his things and leave me alone. I told him I was going to Georgia and I was not taking any man with me unless I was married to him.

That is when he came back with a ring. When he proposed, his sister was in the background yelling no. I did not care. The proposal was not about romance. It was about choice. He chose to stay. He chose to grow. He chose to be accountable.

Nakia had his demons. Drinking. Pills. Lying. Generational habits he had never been taught how to break. But unlike the men before him, he respected my gift. And every time he tried to lie or cheat, my discernment exposed him. Not to shame him, but to force growth.

We grew together. We healed together. We struggled together. We faced homelessness, constant moving, stress, setbacks, and moments where life felt like it was trying to break us in half. But we never left each other standing alone.

I had been with men who had money but no soul. Men with status but no loyalty. Nakia did not have the extras, but he had a heart that stayed beside mine when life was trying to kill me.

In 2019, we got married. Not because it was a fairy tale. Because it was real.

He was not just my husband. He became my partner. My co-owner. My production partner. My support system. The man who learned how to love a woman with a gift instead of trying to control it.

Nakia did not save me. He just stood with me while I saved myself.

Chapter 19
Returning to Myself

For so long, I had become versions of myself based on survival — versions built from trauma, fear, motherhood, and struggle. But in my late 20s and early 30s, something shifted.

I started returning to myself. The real me. The spiritual me. The gifted me. The woman God designed before the world tried to break her.

I began listening to my intuition again, that inner voice that always knew danger, always predicted betrayal, always warned me when something was wrong. I stopped hiding my gift to make others comfortable. I stopped denying my visions and spiritual encounters. I stopped apologizing for the power God placed in me.

My gift wasn't a burden; it was my armor, my direction, my divine compass. And as I stepped back into myself, opportunities began opening, not because life got easier, but because I finally aligned with who I was supposed to be.

The world couldn't dim me anymore. I refused to shrink. I refused to be silent. I refused to be anything less than chosen.

Chapter 20
My Spiritual Business
Awakens (2019)

2019 was the year everything shifted. For years, I had hidden my gift: the visions, the messages, the dreams, the ability to communicate with the deceased, the intuition that saw through lies.

People feared what I could see. Some used me. Some drained me. Some only came when they wanted free readings or temporary help.

But that year, I stopped hiding my gift from the world. I stepped into my purpose publicly. I launched my spiritual business. I let people witness the accuracy of my visions. I helped strangers find answers. I guided souls through heartbreak, confusion, and loss.

My online presence grew. My spiritual readings gained attention. People began recognizing the authenticity in my gift.

The work was heavy, even draining at times, but powerful. My gift wasn't entertainment; it was divine. And the more I embraced it, the more doors began to open in business, creativity, and destiny.

That year became the foundation for everything I would build after: the store, the ministry, the films, the empire.

My gift deepened as I grew older.

I didn't ask to speak with the deceased. I didn't ask to see visions. I didn't ask to feel the emotions of spirits passing through. It was simply a calling placed on me since age four.

The dead speak — not in screams, but in whispers. They show their past. They reveal the truth. They guide. They warn. They seek closure.

Some nights, I saw flashes of people's final moments. Some days, I felt the emotions of spirits who refused to leave until their message was heard.

This gift weighed heavy. It made relationships complicated. People wanted my insight but didn't want my truth. They liked my gift when it benefited them, but rejected me when it exposed things they didn't want revealed.

But I learned something powerful: My gift is not for entertainment. It is for protection, guidance, and purpose. It saved lives. It exposed lies. It revealed destiny. It helped souls cross over. It protected me from men who meant me harm. It directed me toward the path that built my empire.

People tried to silence me, drain me, take advantage of me, but destiny doesn't bend to jealousy. It doesn't break under envy. It doesn't shrink for fear.

My calling was bigger than people's opinions, and the more I embraced it, the more unstoppable I became.

Chapter 21
The Business, The Spiritual Work & Becoming Black Magic

People don't understand spiritual gifts until they need you. Until they're crying on your porch at 2 AM. Until they're begging you to pray, to read, to pull them out of the darkness that life shoved them into.

My spiritual work wasn't something I picked up; it picked me at four years old. I turned my pain into purpose. I turned my survival into a calling. And I turned my calling into a business.

Black Magic Productions didn't start as a cute name; it started as my real power, my real identity, my real story. I built spiritual work, products, protection oils, mojo bags, services, and a following that trusted the gift in me because they saw it change lives.

Then Nakia stepped in beside me, learning, helping, watching, supporting. At first, he didn't understand autism, bipolar episodes, spiritual attacks, or how deep my gift went. But he learned. He grew with me, not against me.

We built the business from the ground up while life kept trying to tear everything down. People betrayed me. They stole from me. They envied me. They used me.

But baby, my gift never failed me.

Chapter 22
Healing Hands Outreach Ministries – The Calling I Couldn't Run From

I opened my church because God told me to. Not because I wanted to be a pastor, not because I wanted a title, not because I wanted followers.

It was obedience. Pure obedience.

Healing Hands Outreach Ministries became a lifeline for people who had nobody else. I fed, prayed, helped, and poured into people even when I didn't have enough for myself.

My nonprofit never got funded because jealousy blocked blessings that other people could have received. People wanted to see me struggle rather than see me help others.

But I still gave. I still prayed. I still helped every person God sent.

One day, I will build the shelter I dream of for abandoned women, homeless families, and people who need a place to go when life hits them the hardest.

That calling never left me. It just grew.

Chapter 23
Order of the Eastern Star
(2024)

In 2024, another unexpected chapter unfolded — my journey stepped into the Order of the Eastern Star. It was a calling that felt spiritual, ancestral, and aligned.

I joined alongside Andrea, Patricia, and Jessica. The sisterhood felt powerful at first — a place of structure, ritual, and discipline. But I quickly learned that titles attract jealousy.

While some sisters respected me, others envied my light, my gift, my knowledge, and the speed at which I elevated.

Still, I embraced the lessons. I participated. I prayed. I learned the sacred meanings behind the symbols. I fulfilled my part with dignity.

The experience taught me how to stand firm in rooms with hidden jealousy, how to carry myself with grace, how to spiritually protect myself from envious energies, and how to lead even when others want you to dim your light.

The Eastern Star journey didn't last forever, but it strengthened my leadership, my discipline, and my spirit.

Chapter 24
At Your Grave Site (Film #1)

While people sometimes mix the titles, *At Your Grave Site* and *Praying At Your Grave Site* were two separate films, each with its own purpose, message, and storyline.

At Your Grave Site was my very first film surrounding the theme of death, grief, and spiritual messages. It told the story of how one visit to a grave can unravel truths people hide for years.

In this film:

- A character discovered secrets buried with a loved one.
- Family lies were exposed.
- Spirits appeared in visions.
- Past relationships resurfaced.
- Emotional closure became the only path forward.

This movie was the spark that lit the rest of my spiritual film journey. It gave me the confidence to create on a deeper, more emotional level, and it was the first time I realized how much my films could heal real people.

At Your Grave Site was raw, passionate, authentic, and a testimony to how the spiritual world guides me creatively.

Chapter 25
The Actors Who Betrayed Me

Success doesn't just attract supporters; it also exposes the snakes. Some of the people I gave opportunities to — people I trusted, believed in, supported, clothed, fed, booked, and elevated — turned out to be ungrateful, jealous, and disloyal.

They tried to use my:

- creativity
- resources
- platform
- kindness

without giving loyalty in return.

Some tried to sabotage my productions. Some tried to take control of ideas they didn't create. Some talked behind my back while smiling in my face. Some tried to outshine me using the shine I gave them. One or two even tried to tear me down on social media.

But the truth always surfaced. My gift revealed every betrayal before they even acted on it. And instead of breaking me, the betrayal only made me better.

I replaced them with real talent. I elevated new actors. I removed toxic energy from my sets. I continued producing bigger and better projects.

Their betrayal became their curse. My growth became my revenge.

Chapter 26
Louisiana Store & New Orleans Connections

Louisiana changed everything.

In the process of making the film Inside my House 2, the mask fell off, the videographer was a complete scammer. He took money and didn't produce final clips of my movie. After leaving the scammers and manipulators in Memphis behind, I built something new in Louisiana — a spiritual store mixed with film production dreams. It was there that I found strangers who treated me better than people I'd known for years.

A friend introduced me to a whole new world of support, and through that connection, I met people from New Orleans who became a major part of my journey.

They didn't just work with me; they respected me. They honored my vision. They understood my gift. They valued my presence. We filmed. We planned. We grew as a team.

My Louisiana store became a safe haven for customers and a spiritual workspace for film inspiration. I did readings, made products, prayed with people, and created a foundation that would later fuel my film projects.

I was a Memphis girl building a Louisiana legacy —proof that your roots don't limit your reach.

Chapter 27
Inside My House 2 – Louisiana, New Faces & The Real Breakthrough

By the time I moved to Louisiana, life had shifted again.

I met Vincent, a man who became a lifelong friend and advisor. He believed in me when I barely believed in myself. He did the print and press and helped me with my clothing line.

Then I met Hollywood Pompeii Studios — people who treated me like family. Jade, Seven, Terrion, and Jay — men who respected my gift, my work ethic, my vision, and my talent.

We shot Mirrored Marriage, that's also where I met Kidd Kidd, a legendary artist who became part of our circle and respected my grind.

Louisiana gave me a new family, new opportunities, and showed me who was real and who just wanted to eat off my gift.

Chapter 28
My Liquor Line

One of the boldest moves I ever made was creating my own liquor line, not one flavor, but multiple.

Vodqilla became its own brand:

- Black Tropical
- Black Green Lime
- Black Strawberries and Cream
- (and others in development)

These drinks represented:

- luxury
- boldness
- empowerment
- Black-owned success
- creativity
- entrepreneurial independence

I designed the bottles, the labels, the concept — all with *Black Magic* excellence.

Just like everything else I built, the liquor line came from nothing but vision and determination. It wasn't easy. Licensing, branding, testing, dealing with vendors — it was all a challenge.

But every obstacle reminded me why it mattered: To build something that would live beyond me. The liquor line became a symbol of leveling up — proof that my brand wasn't just spiritual, not just cinematic, but generational.

Chapter 29
The Mississippi Scam, The Possession & Coming Back Home

After Louisiana, we moved to a house in Mississippi — Corey Taylor's place. A liar. A manipulator. A man who promised help, renovations, support, and peace, and delivered none of it.

The house was falling apart, dangerous, and spiritually contaminated. I became possessed in that house, by demons, the energy, the trauma, and the spiritual war happening in those walls.

We left everything behind to save our lives. We came back to Memphis — broke, tired, traumatized — and I opened my store.

But that store? Cursed. Everything fought against me in there. Nothing went right. Nothing flowed. Nothing felt blessed. We left that, too. Walked away before it destroyed us.

I found us another house — a good house — after another scam tried to break us. And that's when everything finally shifted.

Chapter 30
My Clothing Line

Creativity flows through every part of my spirit —from films, to music, to spiritual products, and into fashion.

My clothing line was born from:

- my brand
- my style
- my vision
- my spiritual identity

I created:

- spiritual glam designs
- brand shirts
- hoodies
- dresses
- pants sets
- empire-themed outfits
- character shirts from my movies
- Black Magic gear for supporters
- bold, powerful fashion representing strength

Some pieces were dramatic and glam; some were simple but meaningful. Every item carried the energy of a woman who survived hell and created heaven with her own hands.

The clothing line wasn't just fabric; it was storytelling. It was empowerment. It was a declaration that my brand lives in every form of expression.

Chapter 31
Nakia's Family's Jealousy & My Strength

Loving Nakia was one thing. Dealing with his family was another.

Jealousy is a powerful poison, especially when it comes from people who should love you. Some laughed behind my back. Some whispered about me. Some hated the spiritual gift God gave me because they feared what it revealed.

His mother smiled, but her spirit wasn't aligned with mine. She accepted my help but refused to accept me. She lied. She manipulated. She stirred drama that never needed to exist. She even agreed to make my wedding dress, took money, and produced nothing but excuses.

Others in his family followed her lead, adding fuel to fires that didn't need to burn. But through every insult, every lie, every attempt to break us apart, Nakia never left.

Their jealousy only strengthened my spirit. It made me pray harder, stand firmer, and understand my worth more deeply.

People can interfere with a relationship, but they cannot stop a connection God designed.

Chapter 32
The Herbal Store & Spiritual Line

My spiritual business didn't stop at readings, visions, and prophecies. It grew into something bigger, something tangible, something healing, something people could physically hold onto.

I launched my herbal and spiritual product line:

- Home-blessed soaps
- Herbal lotions
- Protection oils
- Spiritual oils
- Attraction oils
- Cleansing sprays
- Candles charged with intention
- Hair-growth oils
- Lip glosses
- Car diffusers and spiritual scents
- Custom spiritual kits
- Body butters
- Fragrance blends made from herbs and intuition

Every product was crafted from prayer, spiritual alignment, and knowledge passed down through my gift.

I didn't just make items; I activated them. People came for spiritual healing. They came for results. They came because my work worked. And with every order, every testimony, every transformation, I saw my purpose expanding.

My store — first in Memphis (2023), then in Louisiana — became a place of refuge. A place where people came broken and left lighter. A place where ancestors guided my hands as I prepared each item.

Even when the storefront struggled financially, I continued. Why? Because it wasn't just business; it was ministry, healing, and spiritual responsibility. The herbal line became one of the early cornerstones of my empire.

Chapter 33
Seven Movies in Sixteen Months

Most people can't film one movie in a year. Most indie creators struggle with funding, actors, locations, or support. But with God's strength, my gift, and unstoppable determination, I filmed seven movies in less than sixteen months.

Every day felt like a battle and a blessing at the same time. I didn't have big budgets. I didn't have Hollywood cameras. I didn't have million-dollar investors. What I had was vision and a team that believed in me enough to show up.

Some days, we filmed in intense heat. Some days, we filmed in freezing cold. Some days, actors didn't show up. Some days, scenes had to be rewritten on the spot.

But we kept going.

I cried between takes. I laughed between shots. I fought spiritual battles while holding the camera. And through it all, we produced movies that touched hearts, opened eyes, and told stories that needed to be heard.

Seven films. Seven testimonies. Seven pieces of my soul on screen.

Every movie was a prayer answered. Every script was a deliverance. Every premiere was a reminder that God rewards persistence.

Chapter 34
Inside My House (Film #2)

Inside My House was the film that started it all — the foundation of *Black Magic Productions.* It was raw, emotional, spiritual, and bold. This movie told the truth about what happens when demons don't just enter a home physically… but spiritually. Inspired by real-life trauma and betrayal, the film explored hidden relationships, family problems, and the spiritual warfare that goes on behind closed doors.

We filmed it with limited resources and maximum heart. The cast brought their full selves. The emotions were real. The storyline hit home for so many viewers.

People cried watching it. People messaged me saying it felt like I was telling their story, too. People finally understood the type of storyteller I was — authentic, fearless, spiritually driven.

Inside My House wasn't just a film. It was the birth of my cinematic identity.

Chapter 35
Inside My House 2 (Film #3)

The first film was powerful, but *Inside My House 2* elevated it even further. This sequel carried more profound emotion, darker secrets, and more intense spiritual warfare. It followed characters through generational trauma, deception, heartbreak, and deliverance.

I incorporated my gift into the writing — visions, intuition, messages from the spiritual realm — because real life is spiritual, and so are the stories I tell.

This film carried themes of redemption, betrayal, revelation, and battles of the mind. The actors brought their best performances. Nakia stepped deeper into his role behind the scenes, co-directing and visually capturing the story.

By the time we finished the final scene, I knew this movie was waste of money and time . It showed my growth as a director, writer, and leader, and it proved that sequels can be even stronger than the originals.

Chapter 36
Mirrored Marriage (Film #4)

This film was about a couple on the run who were forced to stop running.

A police chase had driven them across state lines, leaving them exhausted, desperate, and in need of a place to disappear. When they reached Louisiana, escape was no longer an option. They needed shelter, stability, and time—something that felt impossible given the circumstances.

By chance, or what felt like fate, they came across a home left behind by a military couple who had recently been relocated. The resemblance between the two couples was striking, almost unsettling, as if their lives were reflecting one another. It seemed like the perfect solution—a ready-made refuge where they could settle quietly and rebuild.

However, the illusion of safety didn't last long.

The house came with overwhelming costs and constant upkeep they couldn't afford, turning what appeared to be a blessing into another burden. Things grew more complicated when it was revealed that the military couple were also pastors. Once the local pastors discovered this connection, old habits and hidden agendas resurfaced. What began as hospitality quickly shifted into manipulation and quiet scheming.

The couple realized they had escaped one kind of pursuit only to fall into another—one rooted in power, control, and appearances rather than law enforcement. The film explores how desperation can push people into unfamiliar roles, and how faith, when mixed with ambition, can become just as dangerous as any weapon.

Mirrored Marriage was ultimately about identity, survival, and the unsettling realization that sometimes the most threatening traps are the ones that look like salvation.

Chapter 37
Within A Blink (Film #5)

This film took an unexpected turn—it was a story about how life can change in a blink. I wanted viewers to feel just how fragile normalcy is, how quickly fate, danger, love, or tragedy can collide. One moment everything feels familiar and safe, and the next, the ground shifts beneath your feet.

The story centers on a married couple longing to start a family. They want a baby, but the timing never seems right. Deniece is ready for motherhood and eager to seize every opportunity life offers, while her husband is constantly consumed by work, convinced that providing comes before everything else. Their lives move in parallel but rarely intersect, and the emotional distance between them quietly grows.

Trying to ease the guilt of his absence, her husband sends Deniece on a shopping spree—thinking that gifts might fill the space he can't. It's during one of these outings that everything changes. Deniece notices a small dog wandering alone, unaccompanied and vulnerable. Acting on impulse rather than reason, she takes the dog, convincing herself she's rescuing it.

But within a blink, that single decision spirals out of control.

The dog's owner is far from ordinary—unstable, obsessive, and relentless. She manages to catch Deniece's license plate and tracks her down to her home. What follows is an explosive confrontation that turns physical and chaotic, drawing the attention of neighbors and ultimately the police.

As authorities get involved, tensions rise and loyalties crack. The most unexpected people step forward as informants, proving that danger doesn't always come from strangers—sometimes it comes from those closest to you.

Within a Blink is a reminder that life doesn't always unravel slowly. Sometimes, everything changes in an instant, and one small choice can alter the course of love, safety, and trust forever.

Chapter 38
Escaping The Bubble (Film#6)

Escaping the Bubble was a story about breaking free from comfort zones, toxic cycles, mental prisons, and generational curses. The "bubble" represented everything that traps people emotionally:

- cycles of poverty
- abusive relationships
- jealousy-filled environments
- family dysfunction
- inner fear
- lack of self-worth

Every character in the film struggled with their own bubble. Some fought to break out. Some were too afraid. Some didn't even know they were trapped.

This movie was powerful because it mirrored real life so closely. People get so used to dysfunction that they think it's normal. They get comfortable with misery because it's familiar. They stay stuck because freedom feels scary.

But the truth is: you cannot grow inside a bubble. The film's message was clear: escape before the bubble becomes your coffin.

Production was emotional. The cast poured their hearts into every scene. The storyline touched viewers who had been stuck in their own bubbles for years. And for me, this movie symbolized my own escape from old relationships, toxic energies, and spiritual battles meant to destroy me.

Chapter 39
Praying At Your Grave Site
(Film #7)

This film carried spiritual weight beyond anything I had written before. *Praying at Your Grave Site* was inspired by real experiences — the pain of loss, the power of closure, and the connection between the living and the dead.

In this story, characters revisited graves to seek answers, offer forgiveness, confront the ghosts of their past (literally and spiritually), and release burdens they had carried for years.

The film explored:

- speaking to ancestors
- spiritual visions
- unfinished business
- hidden family secrets
- emotional healing
- grief
- generational pain
- spiritual callings

This movie showcased my gift more openly — the ability to communicate with spirits, interpret messages, and understand what the deceased still needed to say.

Many people cried watching it. Many reached out to tell me it helped them heal wounds they'd never spoken about. Many said it brought them peace about their own loved ones.

This film wasn't entertainment; it was deliverance.

Chapter 40
The Roku Channel: Black Magic TV

Every empire needs a platform, and God made sure mine had one. Launching *Black Magic Productions TV* on Roku was one of my biggest accomplishments.

I didn't buy a spot on someone else's channel. I bought my own. *Black Magic TV* became the home for:

- All seven films
- Black Couch Interviews
- Mic Drops
- Behind-the-scenes episodes
- Trailers
- Creator spotlights
- Special features
- Future documentaries
- More upcoming series

Seeing my brand on a global streaming platform was surreal. It proved that I wasn't just a local creator; I was a visionary with reach.

People streamed my work from states I've never visited. Families watched my films together. Supporters replayed interviews and episodes. Actors I gave opportunities to sent screenshots of themselves on TV screens.

The Roku channel solidified my production company as a real force — not just an idea, not just an experiment, but a streaming network with my name on it. This chapter in my journey taught me: I am unstoppable.

Chapter 41
Black Couch Interviews

Black Magic Productions wasn't just about films; it was about giving people a platform to speak. That's where *Black Couch Interviews* came from.

I created a space where:

- artists
- actors
- entrepreneurs
- everyday people with powerful stories
- survivors
- creators
- dreamers

could sit down, talk their truth, share their journey, and be seen.

The black couch became a symbol. People sat on it and opened their souls. Conversations were real — no scripts, no edits, no filters.

Some cried. Some laughed. Some confessed. Some healed.

Black Couch Interviews became a signature piece of *Black Magic Productions* — a place where authenticity lived. And it showed that storytelling didn't just happen in movies; it happened face to face, heart to heart.

Chapter 42
Mic Drops

Where *Black Couch Interviews* allowed people to reveal, *Mic Drops* allowed people to express.

This show was all about:

- raw emotion
- bold truth
- music
- speeches
- confessions
- open letters
- personal revelations
- rants
- spoken word
- declarations to the world

People stood in front of the camera, held the mic, and dropped whatever they needed to let go of.

Mic Drops became a community favorite because it gave space for:

- anger to be released
- pain to be spoken
- artists to shine
- people to reclaim their voice

No judgment. No fakeness. No hiding. Just truth.

Mic Drops expanded *Black Magic Productions* into a full media brand — not just films, but expression, communication, healing, and realness.

Chapter 43
Working With Family & Friends

Working with family and friends can be a blessing or a hurricane. Some stepped in with love. Some stepped in with jealousy. Some stepped in with laziness. Some stepped in only thinking that opportunity meant ownership. Some stepped in with genuine support.

I learned very quickly: Blood doesn't always mean loyalty. And friendship doesn't always mean alignment.

But there were also people who showed up for me in ways I will never forget.

Patricia — loyal, real, always listening, always protecting.

Andrea — a true supporter, a motivator, and one of the most consistent energies around me.

Latoya — trustworthy, grounded, and present.

Jessica — a sister in the Eastern Star journey with me.

Tony — a friend who supported me from day one.

And my kids — even if they didn't always understand my gift, even if life pulled them in different directions, they were my reason, my motivation, my heart.

Working with family and friends wasn't easy, but it taught me discernment, patience, boundaries, and appreciation for the few who truly stood in my corner.

Chapter 44
The Weight Of My Calling

I never thought my gift would feel like a burden. Not at first, at least. I thought it was meant to heal, to lift, to bring light to the people who needed me. But as I got deeper into my spiritual work, I realized there's a price to carrying a gift like mine.

Some of that price is invisible. Some of it is spiritual. Some of it hits you in ways that money or sleep or comfort never can.

There were nights when I barely slept. I would lie in bed, heart pounding, mind racing, sensing things around me that I couldn't see. I felt energies that weren't mine trying to latch onto me. Some people who came to me for help carried spirits I could feel, even before they spoke a word. Their pain was heavy, yes, but so was the darkness that followed them. I had to fight it for them. I had to fight it for myself. And it drained me more than any sleepless night, more than any financial struggle, more than the jealousy of people who didn't want me to rise.

And then there was the decline—the loss of income, the people who stopped paying after receiving my work, the friends who disappeared. I started asking myself if this was a curse or a gift. If all of this loss, all of this exhaustion, was punishment or preparation. I questioned whether I had stretched myself too far, given too much, prayed too hard. I wondered if my spiritual gift was worth the toll it was taking.

I prayed more than ever. I prayed through the night when sleep abandoned me. I prayed through every ache in my body and every fear in my heart. I prayed for protection, for guidance, for wisdom. I prayed for God to remove the dark forces that tried to attach themselves to me, my business, and my life. Some nights, I shouted the prayers into the quiet of my room, demanding release, demanding freedom, demanding that nothing unholy should cling to me. Sweat would run down my back, tears would soak my pillow, and my body would tremble, but my spirit stood firm.

And then I made a deal with God. I whispered it quietly, but with certainty:

"If You remove the darkness, I will walk fully in the empire You are building through me. I will accept the responsibility, even if it costs me everything. Clear my path so I can grow financially and spiritually."

That was my turning point. Not instant, not dramatic, not without struggle—but it shifted everything. The people I prayed for began leaving my life. Not because I forced them out, but because their energy couldn't survive in my cleared space. Some never even realized it, some resented it, some blamed me, but I felt relief. I gained room to breathe. I gained the space I needed to grow.

Even as my income dropped, even as my sleep became thinner, even as the world seemed to misunderstand me, I knew I had made the right choice. The decline wasn't a punishment; it was a divine clearing.

God was stripping away everything that couldn't rise with me. Every person who left, every client who disappeared, every dollar that didn't come in—it was removing the weight that would have held my gift back.

And slowly, I began to feel it. A subtle shift. My intuition sharpened. I could sense intentions more clearly. I could feel truth and deception as tangibly as a breeze on my skin. I could see the difference between those who truly wanted healing and those who were only there to take from me. My body might have been exhausted, but my spirit was awakening in ways I hadn't yet imagined.

I realized then that this was the price of purpose. The late nights, the financial setbacks, the spiritual battles—they weren't breaking me. They were refining me. They were preparing me for the empire I had only dreamed of. The empire that would not just sustain me, but bless countless others in ways I could not yet see.

Every night I had prayed, every battle I had fought, every loss I had endured—it was all shaping me. My gift wasn't a curse, and though the road was lonely, though the world often didn't understand, I stayed faithful. I stayed committed. I stayed in prayer.

Because I knew, deep in my soul, that my empire was rising, and nothing—not darkness, not jealousy, not lost income, not exhaustion—would stop it.

But they don't see the woman behind it all.

The woman who survived:

- childhood instability
- teen motherhood
- three marriages before real love
- rape
- kidnapping
- homelessness

- hotel living
- spiritual attacks
- abusel
- betrayal
- poverty
- judgment
- jealousy
- manipulation
- losing herself
- rebuilding herself
- fighting demons
- healing others
- carrying gifts she never asked for
- the private tears
- the late-night prayers
- the sacrifices
- the battles

They don't see the strength it took to stand again after so many people tried to break me. I am the woman behind the brand, but the brand did not create me. The struggle did. God did.

Chapter 45
Building My Empire In Faith

Every morning I wake up, I remind myself that this empire isn't built with just my hands; it's built with my faith, my prayers, and my willingness to stay the course even when the world doesn't make sense.

I've learned that faith isn't just a word; it's an action. It's waking up every morning and choosing to believe that the decline isn't the end. It's choosing to pray when the enemy seems louder than the blessing. It's choosing to keep going even when no one is cheering me on.

Faith is persistence. Faith is endurance. Faith is knowing that the invisible forces at work are shaping me for something bigger than I can see.

And patience... oh, patience has been the hardest lesson of all. I've wanted results immediately. I've wanted recognition, income, and validation yesterday. But God doesn't work on our schedule; He works on His.

I've learned to wait. To trust. To remain steady even when the path seems unclear. Prayer has become my lifeline. It's no longer just words; I speak with authority. I call out darkness when it tries to touch me or my work. I ask for protection, guidance, clarity, and the removal of anything that would prevent me from growing. I pray not just for myself, but for the people I serve. I pray that the work I do touches hearts, that the movies and TV content I create inspire, educate, and help others follow their own dreams. Each prayer fuels me, strengthens me, and reminds me that

I am never alone in this journey.

I've also learned that helping others is part of my own growth. My empire isn't just about money or recognition; it's about creating opportunities for others to rise. Every movie I produce, every TV channel segment I plan, every story I tell carries the intention of inspiring others. I want people to see that dreams are possible, that spiritual gifts can coexist with business, and that, with faith and persistence, they, too, can overcome obstacles.

Helping others pursue their passions feeds my spirit in ways money never could. It reminds me why I started this journey, and it gives every sacrifice a purpose.

I've learned to release control while staying fully engaged in the work I am called to do. I've seen growth I didn't expect. My income is beginning to stabilize, the right clients are coming in, and the people who are meant to walk this path with me are stepping forward. My gift is becoming more recognized, not because I chase approval, but because I stay consistent, faithful, and patient. I am learning that success is not only about what I create but also about the legacy I leave—the impact I have on others' lives, the inspiration I provide, and the doors I open for those who follow their dreams.

I can finally say that I am not defined by the struggles I endured. I am defined by the faith I held, the patience I practiced, and the prayers I never stopped lifting. My empire is more than buildings or money; it is the manifestation of my gift, my perseverance, and my heart for others.

And now, nothing can stop me.

Chapter 46
Rebuilding With Purpose

The morning air felt heavy with expectation as I sat at my desk, staring at the scattered papers, and countless notes of ideas for my TV channel and spiritual projects. The last few months had been exhausting. My energy was drained, my body begged for rest, but my spirit refused to quit.

I reminded myself why I had started this journey. It wasn't about fame, recognition, or even immediate financial reward. My calling was about purpose—lifting others with my gift, creating platforms that inspired dreams, and showing that persistence, prayer, and faith could overcome the heaviest of obstacles.

With that thought, I lifted my pen and began writing again, not caring that my hands shook from fatigue or that the room was quiet except for the hum of the city outside my window.

The first steps in rebuilding were small but deliberate. I reviewed every client, every unfinished project, every idea that had been abandoned or delayed. I prayed over them all, asking God for clarity on where to invest my energy.

One of the most difficult parts of rebuilding was confronting my own doubt. I had been taught that gifts like mine are rare and powerful, but they are also targets. But each time I doubted, I remembered the covenant I had made with God: *"Remove the darkness from my path, guide me, and I will persist."* That promise anchored me.

I took breaks to reflect and meditate, recognizing that rebuilding was not just practical; it was spiritual. I reminded myself that every setback had a lesson.

By evening, I called my husband to discuss the next steps, sharing both the progress and the challenges. He reminded me that faith and patience were as important as strategy.

"Ginger," he said, "you've built this with prayer, persistence, and integrity. Don't let the setbacks define you. Let them refine you." His words hit me with the force I needed. They reminded me that I was not alone, and that the few people who truly believed in me were worth more than any number of temporary followers.

The process of rebuilding with purpose taught me that success is never linear; it is layered with struggle, spiritual growth, insight, and alignment.

As I finally laid my pen down and prepared for rest, I felt a sense of peace settle over me. The day had been long, and yet, I could feel the quiet pulse of momentum starting to grow. I had begun rebuilding, not just for survival, but for the fulfillment of my calling. And I knew that persistence, prayer, and purpose would guide every step forward.

Epilogue
My Message to The World

If you read this story, lived through these pages with me, felt the pain, the fire, the strength, the victories... then hear me clearly:

Your past does not disqualify you. Your trauma does not define you. Your pain is not your punishment; it is your preparation. Everything you survived has shaped your destiny. Everything you lost has made room for what was coming. Everything you feared has become your testimony.

I want the world, especially Black women, to understand:

You can survive abuse. You can survive betrayal. You can survive broken families. You can survive rape. You can survive poverty. You can survive heartbreak. You can survive anything and still build an empire.

My life is proof.

I came from instability, violence, struggle, and abandonment, and I became a CEO, a business owner, a spiritual leader, a film director, a producer, a musician, a creator, a healer, a wife, a mother, a grandmother, and a woman of power.

The world tried to bury me, but they didn't know I was planted.

To everyone reading this:

Rise. Heal. Build. Transform. Create. Believe. Become.

Because the gift within you, just like the gift within me, was never meant to stay hidden.

This is my story. My legacy. My truth. My empire.

I am Ginger Deniece Pittman.

Black Magic Productions is mine.

The empire is mine.

The legacy is mine.

The gift within me will live forever.

And I'm just getting started.

About the Author

Ginger Deniece Pittman was born on April 4, 1977, at 4:00 AM, weighing 4 pounds, 4 ounces, to Vernnell Cleaves (now Vernnell Harvey) and Karl L. Cleaves. Raised within a blended but deeply connected family, Ginger is the proud sister of Faye, Pamela, sister to Maurice, Aariona, Kristy, Karl Jr.,and Kristopher and Danielle (sister by love).

She is the devoted mother of three children — Karderius, Keonna, and Kywra — and the loving grandmother of three beautiful grandbabies: Khy'lan, Kai'den, and Ka'Mari, who inspire her spirit every day.

Ginger is the CEO, Founder, and Owner of *Black Magic Productions*, and the wife of Nakia Pittman, her partner in life, love, and empire-building. Through pain, survival, spiritual awakening, and unstoppable determination, she transformed her struggles into strength and built an empire rooted in faith, family, and purpose.

My Gift My Purpose

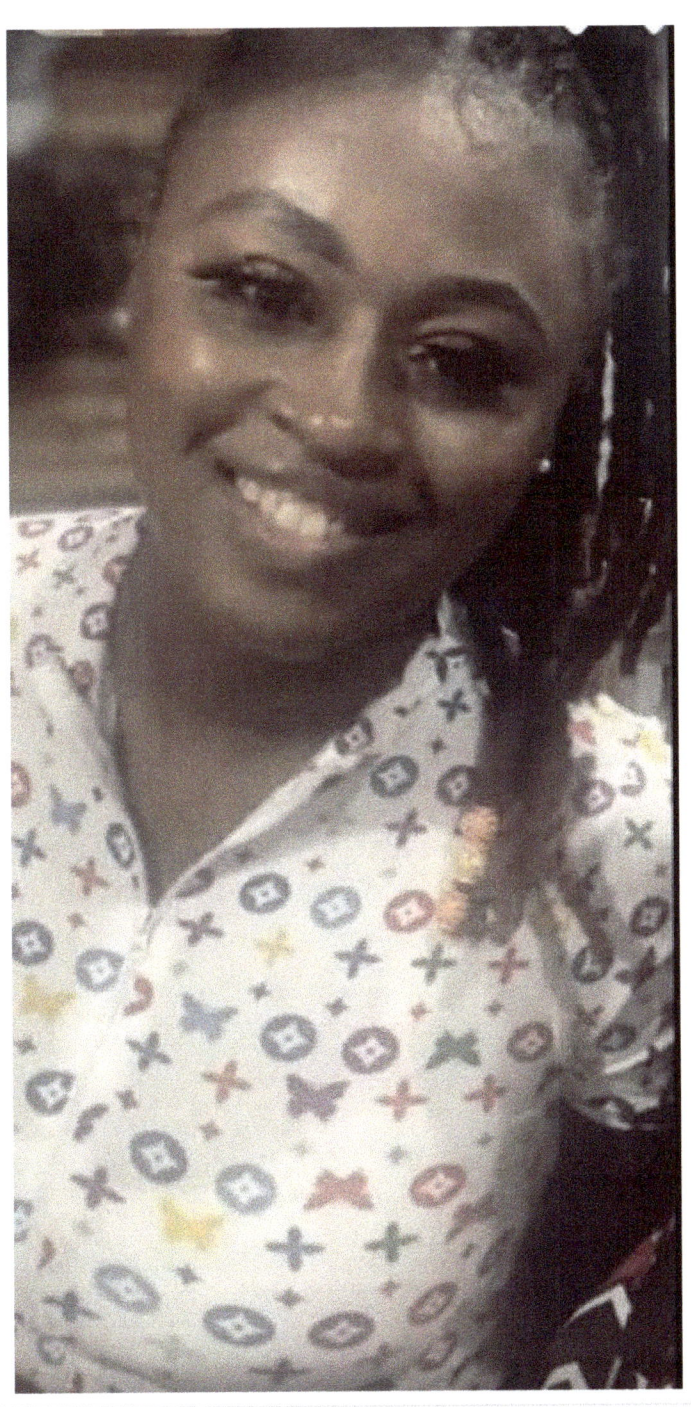

www.ingramcontent.com/pod-product-compliance
Lightning Source LLC
Chambersburg PA
CBHW051221120626
46547CB00013B/1449